The Storm and the Samurai

Written by Nadine Cowan

Illustrated by Nadine Cowan and Katie Crumpton

Collins

CHAPTER 1

Aniyah bounded through the doors of Blue Mahoes restaurant, followed by her cousin EJ and their friend, Olivia. Blue Mahoes was Aniyah and EJ's family restaurant, which had served tasty meals from the Caribbean to their London community for years.

"Admit it! Comic Con was totally epic," EJ brandished a plastic sword in the air and swooshed it about in a swift figure of eight. He swiped the blade through Olivia's hair.

"Hey, watch it! You're not a real samurai!" Olivia said, fixing her cat ears back into place.

"Well, the organisers at Comic Con loved my costume!" EJ replied, pulling out a shiny gold medal. EJ was dressed as a character from his favourite Manga comic, and he'd won first place in the costume competition.

"It was so much fun," Aniyah replied.

EJ smiled. "Yeah. We got to dress up as our favourite comic book characters, and we met some great comic book artists."

There weren't any customers in the restaurant, which meant the lunch-time rush was over. Aniyah headed straight to the fridge and pulled out some cold drinks.

"Which flavour do you want, EJ?" she asked, but EJ wasn't listening. He was sitting at one of the restaurant tables, looking intently at a new comic he'd bought at Comic Con.

"You've had your head buried in that comic since we left Comic Con! I thought we were going to play the Ludi game," Olivia sighed.

EJ stared longingly at the page he was on; it was a story about an African samurai.

He grabbed a drink and sighed, "OK" before following the others downstairs.

The friends sunk down into the couch in the basement room beneath the restaurant. The old wooden Ludi board game was on the table in front of them. It was a family heirloom, and it wasn't just any old board. There were words etched on the side:

Roll double six, or double three,

let's learn about your history.

Whenever the children played the Ludi game, something magical always happened.

When EJ rolled a double six, a puff of iridescent smoke burst from the board and engulfed the children, then a tornado that formed a wormhole pulled them in.

CHAPTER 2

Aniyah felt drops of water hit her face. At first it was one or two drops but suddenly an army of raindrops trampled all over her. She shielded her eyes and looked around for her friends. It didn't take her long to spot them among the trees. Olivia looked bewildered as she stood beside EJ, squeezing the excess water from her clothing. She had a lengthy piece of rope wrapped around one of her shoulders, weighing her down. EJ was looking around, trying to see through the trees. A strong gust of wind blew, forcing Aniyah towards them.

"WOW! Look at your hair! Is my hair
that cool?" Olivia asked Aniyah.
She raised her hands to her head.
Her face lit up when she
felt a hair ornament
poking out. Both girls
had their hair pulled
up into ponytails;
Aniyah's ponytail
formed two circles
on top of her head,
and Olivia's formed
a shapely bun.

"Yes, yes, fancy
hair," EJ said.

White flecks blew
past them in a flurry.

Olivia looked up.
"Is that *snow*?"

"I think it's cherry
blossom," Aniyah said,
and she reached out to grab
the delicate petals.

8

"Where do you think we are?" Aniyah asked.

"A forest!" EJ said.

"Ha ha, very helpful. Not," Olivia replied. "Where is there a forest with cherry trees?"

"No idea," EJ huffed.

"Well," Olivia looked down at her clothing, "these aren't the right clothes for tramping through a forest."

The girls were wearing loose-fitting garments with wide sleeves. Olivia had never worn anything like it.

"It's like a large robe," Aniyah said.

EJ was also wearing a loose-fitting garment. "Look at my trousers!" he laughed.

Olivia thought about dropping the rope she was carrying because it was so heavy, but the Ludi board always provided a useful object when they travelled back in time, and this could be it.

EJ thought the clothing looked familiar, but before he could figure it out another strong gust of wind began to blow around them.

"I think we should find shelter," Aniyah shouted, her voice muffled by the wind.

"Good idea!" Olivia shouted back. The children looked around, but the rain started to fall more heavily and made it hard to see.

EJ spotted a clearing beside some trees. "Over there, let's head that way."

The children began to run towards the clearing, but Olivia couldn't move! She lost her balance and fell straight into the mud.

"Are you OK?" asked Aniyah, as she and EJ reached out and pulled Olivia to her feet.

"It's these shoes! I can't run in them," Olivia sighed, as she dug a wooden sandal out of the mud and held it up. It looked like a flip-flop with stilts on the sole.

Aniyah looked up at the sky and gulped, dark clouds loomed up above.

"Grab them, we need to get out of here quick!" she screamed, as a branch blew past her face.

Olivia grabbed the other shoe, and the children headed for the clearing.

There was an almighty splintering sound as a tall tree crashed down where they'd been standing a moment before.

"W ... What's that?" EJ said, with a wobble in his voice.

Aniyah and Olivia looked back, past the fallen tree. Two bright eyes stared back.

"Run!" screamed Olivia, as a brown bear charged out of the trees.

CHAPTER 3

The children stumbled through the undergrowth, panting heavily.

"Don't look back, don't look back," EJ gasped over and over again.

Suddenly they skidded to a halt. It was a stream!

"We need to get across," Aniyah said, "like, NOW!"

"Look, there's a narrow bridge over there!" shouted EJ.

The wind howled as they ran towards it.

Aniyah went across first, holding her shoes in one hand. She spread out her arms for balance, and carefully placed one foot in front of the other. Just then, another gust of wind blew and she fell to her knees.

Clinging to the bridge, she crawled on her hands and knees to the other side.

"Hands and knees it is!" Olivia said, as she crawled across the bridge after Aniyah. Debris from the wood flew around her and her clothes were wet and heavy, but she made it.

EJ stepped on to the bridge. The river swelled and crashed below, and EJ tried to swallow away the tightness in his throat as he took his first step across. He spread his arms out like aeroplane wings as he tried to keep his balance. He was almost across when he heard a low growl behind him. The bear! As he turned, his foot slipped, and he fell headlong into the river.

EJ thrashed about in the cold water as the current pulled him downstream. He was a strong swimmer and he tried to find something to grab hold of.

Water filled his ears, but he could hear the girls' screams as they ran along the riverbank in pursuit.

Olivia desperately unravelled the rope and tried to throw one end into the water, but they were too far behind and the current was so strong EJ couldn't grab it. He wondered if he'd ever make it back home or just be gobbled up by the stream.

Suddenly, he felt something slap him on the wrist. He reached out and grabbed it – it was the rope! He held on tight and felt himself being pulled slowly towards the riverbank.

Strong arms hoisted EJ out of the water and laid him gently on the ground. EJ let go of the rope and lay there, eyes closed. He'd swallowed quite a lot of the river and he coughed and spluttered.

A strong hand patted him on the back and EJ took a deep breath. When he finally opened his eyes, EJ noticed huge furry boots, way too big to belong to Aniyah or Olivia. Slowly his eyes wandered upwards past the cloth gaiters. Up and up … EJ's mouth opened in surprise when he saw the person who stood before him was a giant with huge shoulders and a large metal face!

CHAPTER 4

EJ quickly clambered to his feet and took a step
back as Aniyah and Olivia scrambled down
the bank towards him. EJ looked at the giant
once more. He was wearing armour made of
lacquered wood, an apron of metal plates sewn
on like roof tiles, and silk gloves. Then he spotted
them … not just one, but two swords protruding
from the giant's waist. EJ couldn't believe his
eyes; it was a real-life samurai!

The samurai handed the rope back to Olivia. Then he reached towards his head and lifted off the metal mask. EJ was relieved to see there was a human behind the face covering.

"Thank you for saving my cousin," said Aniyah.

"I'm glad I could help. What are you young ones doing out here in the storm?" asked the man.

"We got lost," Olivia gulped.

"There's a typhoon coming," the samurai said. "We need to find shelter on higher ground. Quick, follow me!"

The children tried to follow the man as he weaved through the woods, but EJ was exhausted after falling in the river. "I can hardly stand up!" he groaned.

The samurai looked back at them. "I have an idea; we could tie your rope around each of our waists."

"At least I won't have to carry it," Olivia said, pleased.

"And that way we can keep up with you, and none of us will blow away," Aniyah replied.

Olivia handed the rope to the man, and he tied it around each of the children before tying a large section around his own waist.

"We thought we were going to lose you in the stream," Aniyah told EJ.

"I was worried I wouldn't make it back to find out what happens at the end of my new comic!" EJ replied.

"At least we didn't get eaten by that bear," Olivia huffed.

They were very cold, wet and tired by the time they reached a rocky outcrop.

"Look! There's a cave!" Aniyah said, with surprise. "At least it will be dry."

"As long as there isn't anything living in there," EJ joked.

They scrambled over the rocks and into the cave entrance, away from the wind. It was dark inside, so they stayed near the entrance where the daylight crept in and untied the rope from around themselves.

"I suppose we ought to introduce ourselves," Olivia said. They'd been so busy trying to rescue EJ and then tramping through the forest, they didn't even know their rescuer's name. "I'm Olivia, and these are my friends, Aniyah and EJ."

The man stopped untying the rope from around his waist for a moment and lifted his head.

"Kon'nichiwa! Around here most people call me Yasuke."

Kon'nichiwa! thought EJ, who had seen enough anime and read enough Manga to know it meant "hello" in Japanese. He looked again at Yasuke's clothing. Then he looked at his clothing, and the girls'.

"I think we're in Japan!" he said with excitement.

Yasuke laughed. "Of course! You must have swallowed too much water if you've forgotten where you are."

"We absolutely know where we are," Aniyah said, confidently.

Yasuke raised an eyebrow. "From the local village perhaps?"

Olivia smiled. "Yes, that's right."

Yasuke nodded. "I need to find some rocks, sticks, twigs and dried leaves and make a fire. With the winds as strong as they are there should be plenty around here."

"I'll help," said Aniyah. "I bet there are some good rocks in the cave."

"We'll all help; we should stick together," EJ shuddered, as he glanced over to the cave entrance and the darkness beyond.

The children crept further into the cave. EJ felt a twig snap beneath his feet. Crack! He bent down to pick it up and felt a mound of dried leaves. It was very dark; he patted the ground in a circular motion to feel for more.

"There are loads of leaves and sticks down here!" EJ called to Aniyah and Olivia. Aniyah found him in the dark and together they gathered lots of twigs and a huge heap of dried leaves. They'd just started collecting rocks when all of a sudden Olivia let out a scream.

CHAPTER 5

Aniyah and EJ rushed towards the sound.

"Is it the bear?" Aniyah looked around with alarm.

Olivia was hopping about and shaking her long sleeves.

"No! I was picking up a leaf when a humongous beetle crawled over my hand. It almost ate my entire arm! Yuck!"

"Are you talking about this little fella?" EJ picked up a leaf from the ground beside Olivia's feet and held it to her face. A tiny beetle scampered across it and twitched its antenna.

Aniyah felt something flutter past her face.

"I've had enough leaves and twigs, let's get back to Yasuke!" she said firmly.

They gathered up everything and made their way back to the cave entrance.

They found Yasuke beside a giant boulder. He was kneeling on the ground and holding a long stick in his hand. The larger of his two swords rested against the boulder.

"Arigatou!" said Yasuke, as the children lay their findings on the ground beside him and sat down.

"That's 'thank you' in Japanese," EJ whispered to the others.

They watched as Yasuke snapped the long stick in two. Then he rummaged through the rocks that Aniyah had found and chose two rough and ragged ones. He began to pound one against the other, BANG! He struck the rock again, and again until the bigger one had a narrow-pointed edge. Yasuke inspected the sticks once more and began to carve into them until he had one flat piece with a hole and one thin piece.

Yasuke poked the thin stick into the flat piece of wood and began to rotate it between his palms. Smoke began to rise from the wood! Then Yasuke moved the piece of wood and collected the smouldering embers it created.

"Now we need the dried leaves," he said to Olivia.

Olivia gathered the pile of leaves and handed them over. Yasuke dropped the embers into the leaves and began to blow on them. Suddenly a bright orange flame erupted from the dried leaves.

It's like magic, thought Aniyah.

"Now we need to lay the twigs on top, like this," Yasuke explained. The children began to pick up the twigs and place them on top of the flame just like Yasuke had shown them. The flame spread like a game of pass-the-message and soon after it grew into a large fire.

They all huddled around the fire, its flames heating their faces. They felt protected in its warmth as their clothes began to dry.

"Here's some water, have a drink," Yasuke passed the children an earthenware flask and they took turns to have a drink. EJ couldn't contain himself anymore.

"Are you a samurai?"

Yasuke chuckled. "Yes, I am, believe it or not. I haven't been in this country for very long, but I believe I'm the first samurai who's not Japanese."

"*How* did you become a samurai?"

"That's a long story ... but I think we'll be here a while." Yasuke leaned back against the large rock and began to tell his story.

CHAPTER 6

"I arrived in Japan three years ago, in 1579, with a group of Jesuit priests. We'd been sailing for many weeks when our boat docked at Kyoto. It's the largest city in Japan, and home to the Imperial court."

"Did you get seasick?" EJ wanted to know.

Yasuke smiled. "No. I enjoyed sea travel, even though it took me far away from my home in Africa."

"You're a long way from there," Olivia said.

"*We're* a long way from home, too!" Aniyah whispered.

"My job was to protect the priests, and in particular the senior Jesuit, Alessandro," Yasuke continued. "Alessandro was seasick and couldn't wait to get to land. I heard him call the journey 'treacherous' many times."

"What happened after you left the boat?" EJ asked.

Yasuke looked thoughtful. "Well, I made sure Alessandro was safe, and kept my eyes and ears open. I learnt that I was called a 'giant' because I'm so tall – and I don't think many people had seen someone with dark skin like me before."

"But you aren't with the missionaries now, are you?" Olivia said.

"Oh no," Yasuke smiled. "Two years after I arrived, I met someone very important. Oda Nobunaga.

"I know that name!" EJ exclaimed.

Yasuke raised an eyebrow. "So you should, if you're from a local village. Oda Nobunaga is a daimyo, a feudal lord who owns lots of land. He answers to the Shogun, a military ruler appointed by the Emperor of Japan. The Imperial court has made Oda Nobunaga grand minister of state."

"Wow!" EJ's eyes widened. "And you've met him?"

"I have. There are lots of warring factions in Japan – different clans fighting for power – and Oda Nobunaga wants to stop the fighting and unify the country. He's one of the most important men in Japan. If he invites you to meet him, you go!" Yasuke said.

"Did he make you a samurai?" Aniyah asked.

Yasuke laughed. "Not then, no. It took me two years and I had to fight some of his fiercest warriors to prove my strength. But being a samurai isn't just about fighting. Oda Nobunaga was impressed I'd learnt some Japanese, and I displayed some of the other attributes every samurai must have."

"Like what?" EJ wanted to know.

"Our way of life is called Bushido. This is the code every samurai must live by: you must have integrity and value justice. You must have courage and value respect. You must be honest and have honour. You must also be loyal."

EJ nodded.

"Oda Nobunaga invited me to join his clan and gave me a new name – Yasuke. I was given land and, in time, I was rewarded for my loyalty and made a samurai. My katana sword was made especially for me. It's a symbol of the samurai."

"There's a lot more to being a samurai than I thought," EJ said.

Yasuke looked at him. "You're still young. There's time to learn. You too may ride side-by-side with Oda Nobunaga as I did in the battle against the Takeda clan.

CHAPTER 7

"If he arrived in 1579, then it must be 1582 now!'"
Aniyah whispered to Olivia.

"I can't believe EJ wants to be a samurai!" Olivia
whispered back.

EJ was mesmerised by Yasuke's story. Yasuke was just
like the samurai in the comics he loved to read and
the anime he enjoyed watching; in fact, he was certain
the name Oda Nobunaga was in the comic he was
reading before they travelled back in time to 1582.

Yasuke sighed. "I came here to survey the land for
the Oda clan, then the storm started brewing and startled
my horse Senshi and he ran away. I was looking for
Senshi and a place to shelter when I heard Aniyah and
Olivia's screams."

"Oh no! I hope your horse will be OK," gasped Olivia.

"The storm should settle by tomorrow; I will continue
looking for him then."

"We could help you search for him!" said EJ. Aniyah and Olivia agreed.

"Thank you, but rest first." Yasuke reached into his sack and pulled out some blankets. The children spread them out and tried their best to make it as comfortable as possible.

That night Olivia tossed and turned, not because of the lumpy rocks beneath her, but because she couldn't stop thinking about Senshi, lost in the terrible storm.

EJ woke early the next morning. He looked over to the boulder where Yasuke had fallen asleep, but he wasn't there, and neither was his sword. He shook the girls awake.

"Is it morning already? I hardly slept a wink," Olivia said with a massive yawn.

"That was so uncomfortable," Aniyah grumbled.

"Yasuke's gone!" EJ announced.

"Do you think he's gone to look for Senshi?" Olivia asked.

"Maybe he's just left us," Aniyah said.

EJ shook his head. "He's a samurai. There would be no honour leaving us here."

A shadowy figure appeared at the cave entrance and a small rock skipped across the floor. It was Yasuke, and he was holding a large fish.

"You must be hungry!" he said, as he prepared the fire once more.

EJ's stomach rumbled. He would've preferred a bowl of cornflakes with warm milk, or peanut butter on toast, but fish would have to do. Besides, maybe Yasuke would make it into fancy fish fingers.

It wasn't fish fingers.

Yasuke rested his Katana sword on the boulders
again and EJ went over to look at it. He glided his hand
over the hilt, his fingers tracing the grooves of its jewels
and engravings.

"Careful EJ, it's sharp! Only a samurai should handle
a Katana," warned Yasuke.

"I want to be a samurai just like you!" EJ told Yasuke.

"Oh, you do? Being a samurai takes years of training,"
laughed Yasuke.

"I can fight, watch this!" EJ performed a manoeuvre he'd learnt that week at his karate summer camp.

"Not bad," said Yasuke, "but try placing your left leg like this." Yasuke demonstrated with his own left foot planted firmly in the ground.

EJ gave it another go.

"Good! Much better. Keep on training and you'll become a better fighter than me one day," Yasuke said. "But remember, to truly be a samurai, you must follow our way of life – Bushido."

"I can fight and be loyal *and* honourable!" EJ vowed.

They packed up their things and set off to find Senshi. Aniyah slowly stepped out of the cave behind EJ and Olivia and looked out at the view. It was a bright, clear morning and she saw a flock of birds flying in the distance.

They made their way down the side of the mountain and back through the forest, heading to the last place Yasuke was with Senshi before the horse galloped off.

"Senshi!" Yasuke called out, and the children called out too.

All of a sudden, they heard the sound of galloping hooves, and a faint neigh followed by a rustling sound. But it wasn't Senshi. A large horse carrying a fearsome figure in frightening armour appeared. He was accompanied by two other men on foot.

The man on the horse yelled at them, but the children couldn't understand what he was saying. Whatever he said couldn't have been good news because Yasuke sprang into action immediately. He shoved his sack into Olivia's hand and shouted out to the children. "Get back! Run and hide!"

CHAPTER 8

I guess they're not *friends of Yasuke's*, thought EJ, as they ran towards some bushes.

The samurai on horseback raised his bow and arrow and fired. Olivia stumbled and the arrow narrowly missed her ear. The man raised his bow and arrow once more, and this time the arrow shot towards Yasuke. Yasuke sidestepped out of the way just in time. The man then lowered his bow and urged his horse to charge towards Yasuke. Dodging the horse expertly, Yasuke startled it by shouting loudly. The horse reared up and the rider fell off. Yasuke darted forward and brought his Katana down onto the man's helmet and knocked him out.

One of the other samurai ran towards Yasuke, the shiny blade of his sword raised in the air. Yasuke ducked and evaded the man's blows, and their swords clanged.

EJ picked up a stone and threw it at the second man. The man looked towards the bushes.

Aniyah grabbed EJ by the shoulder. "What are you doing? We're supposed to be hiding."

"I just want to help Yasuke!" EJ huffed.

There must be some other way, Aniyah thought. Then she remembered their rope in Yasuke's sack which gave her an idea. She quickly explained what she wanted to do to EJ and Olivia.

As they peered through the bushes they saw Yasuke raise his leg and land a heavy kick to his opponent. The man went flying through the air and landed on his back. The third man raised his sword and ran towards Yasuke.

"Now!" yelled Aniyah.

Olivia and Aniyah held on tightly to one end of the rope while EJ had the other and ran full speed out of the bushes. He dived, skidded and rolled on to his front. Yasuke's opponent never saw it coming, and he yelled as he tripped over the rope and landed on the ground.

Yasuke turned around and butted the man on the head with the side of his sword. The man crumpled to the ground.

"That was ... EPIC!" screamed EJ, as he jumped for joy.

"Epic?" cried Olivia. "More like terrifying!"

Yasuke took the enemy samurai's horse by the reins.

"I'm going to call you Shōri," he said. "We better get moving."

"What about these men?" Aniyah said.

"They'll wake up soon enough," Yasuke replied. "But I'm claiming the horse."

Olivia's shoes had come loose again, so she and Aniyah stopped to fix them. By the time Olivia had finished adjusting them, Yasuke and EJ had disappeared. Ahead was a fork in the path.

"Did you see which way they went?" asked Olivia.

"Uh, no I'm not sure. I think it was that way," Aniyah replied. The girls took the path on the left, but it soon became impassable. Yasuke and EJ were nowhere to be seen.

"I think we took a wrong turn," Aniyah said nervously. Once again, they heard a rustle in the bushes. The girls froze with fear.

Suddenly a large head poked out of the bush. It was another horse! The girls sighed with relief.

"Can you hear that?" Aniyah said. "It sounds like EJ."

"Aniiiiyah! Oliviiiia!"

EJ appeared from the bushes, followed by Yasuke and Shōri.

"You found him! Senshi, you strong horse!" Yasuke chuckled. Upon seeing Yasuke, Senshi let out a snort and headed over to him. Yasuke helped Olivia and Aniyah on to Shōri's back and attached Olivia's rope to her bridle before mounting Senshi and pulling EJ up to sit behind him.

CHAPTER 9

The sun had begun to set, and they'd been riding for some time, when they heard the pounding of hooves heading towards them. Three horses came in to view with three ferocious samurai on their backs.

Not again, thought Olivia.

EJ pulled a face. "I can't do any more running!"

"Yasuke!" cried one of the samurai. Yasuke came to a halt and greeted the men.

"Oh good," EJ sighed. "Friends this time."

"What's wrong?" Yasuke asked.

"It's general Akechi Mitsuhide! He's betrayed us. Lord Oda Nobunaga's life is in danger. The Akechi army are advancing to Kyoto. We must ride to the Honnō-ji temple at once!" explained one of the men.

"Go ahead, I'll follow you," Yasuke replied, his voice urgent.

He turned to the children. "I must go and defend Oda Nobunaga. A battle is no place for you."

"But I want to help!" EJ cried.

"You have helped enough, and for that I thank you," Yasuke told him gently, as he lowered EJ down from Senshi's back. "Stay on this path and you'll arrive at a small village, it will be safer for you there. I really must go!"

Yasuke fixed his metal face covering back on to his head and the children watched as he rode off and disappeared from view.

As they headed towards the small village, a cloud appeared before them. Shōri gave a surprised neigh, but Olivia didn't have time to comfort him. Before she knew it the cloud seized hold of the children and transported them back to their own time.

Aniyah, EJ and Olivia slumped down back on the couch. EJ's comic lay open on the table, just as he'd left it.

"I hope Yasuke will be OK," said Aniyah.

EJ picked up his comic and flicked through the pages.

"I knew it!" EJ cried, showing the page to Aniyah and Olivia.

The illustrations showed Oda Nobunaga on his knees. He was surrounded by fire; his face was filled with dread.

EJ flicked to the very last page, and saw an image of the African samurai, galloping away on a horse. He had escaped!

"I think he'll be just fine!" EJ smiled. "Now come on, it's your turn. Let's play!"

HOW TO BE A SAMURAI

You must help people.

You must be loyal.

You must have courage.

REAL PEOPLE

Yasuke

Not much is known about Yasuke. We *do* know that a tall, African man arrived in Kyoto, Japan, in 1579 and he joined the Oda Nobunaga's clan. In time he trained to become a samurai warrior – the first non-Japanese samurai.

Oda Nobunaga 1534–1582

Oda Nobunaga was a Japanese warrior and government official. He worked to end years of warring between different feudal clans and under his leadership, half of Japan was unified. Not long after his death, the whole of Japan came under one rule.

Akechi Mitsuhide 1528–1582

A samurai general under Oda Nobunaga, Akechi Mitsuhide betrayed his master. Akechi surrounded Oda and his loyal warriors at the temple of Honnō-ji, and his actions led to Oda's death.

Ideas for reading

Written by Gill Matthews
Primary Literacy Consultant

Reading objectives:

- check that the book makes sense to them, discussing their understanding and exploring the meaning of words in context
- predict what might happen from details stated and implied
- summarise the main ideas drawn from more than one paragraph, identifying key details that support the main ideas

Spoken language objectives:

- use relevant strategies to build their vocabulary
- articulate and justify answers, arguments and opinions
- use spoken language to develop understanding through speculating, hypothesising, imagining and exploring ideas

Curriculum links: Relationships education – Caring friendships; Respectful relationships

Interest words: integrity, justice, courage, respect, honest, honour, loyal

Build a context for reading

- Ask children to look closely at the front cover and to read the title. Ask what they think a samurai is.
- Ask them to read the back-cover blurb. Encourage them to predict what the story might be about and to support their predictions with reasons and evidence from the text.

Understand and apply reading strategies

- Read pp2–6 aloud, demonstrating how to use meaning, dialogue and punctuation to read with appropriate expression. Ask children to summarise what has happened in this chapter.
- Children can read pp7–12 and summarise what has happened. Ask where they think the story might be taking place. Explore what they think might happen next.
- Give children the opportunity to read the rest of the story.